Always & NEVER

Malak Morgan

A Simple Message for a Better Life

Publisher: WisdomSpring Publishing
P.O. Box 621101
Oviedo, FL 32762-1101
Paperback edition and Kindle version produced with the permission of the publisher by CreateSpace. www.createspace.com

Printed in the United States of America

Library of Congress Control Number: 2010912467

Paperback ISBN 10: 0-9829483-6-0
Paperback EAN 13: 978-0-9829483-6-1

Always & Never is also available in Kindle version.
eBook ISBN 13: 978-0-9829483-9-2

First Edition: May 19, 2011
Revised Edition: August 3, 2012

To my wife Monica, faithful wife, true gift from God, who showed me another level of faith. I asked God for help, and He sent Monica.

To my son Joseph, who by his smile inspired me to write this work.

To my son Jacob, whose birth motivated me to complete this work.

Acknowledgments

I deeply appreciate the great help and support
provided to me by these two genuine and sincere men:

Dr. Wasfy Mikhael

and

Dr. Mark K. Soliman

Preface

Everyone would like to do the right thing all the time. Every one of us looks for clarity between the right and the wrong. Because of the intermingling of these two areas, most of us fall into that gray area in the middle. This book deals with issues that I noticed in my own life and in the lives of others around me. I would like to share with you the suggestions in this book so that they can help to clarify these issues in your life as they did in my own. I encourage you to mark the ones that touch your heart and ask the Lord to help you adopt them into your life. I encourage you to add suggestions of your own to this book and then pass them on to the generations to come so that they can have a better quality of life based on biblical principles and pure knowledge.

Malak Morgan

Always

1. Always "Trust in the Lord with all your
    heart and lean not on your understanding"
    (Proverbs 3:5).
2. Always have hope in God.
    - Repeat very often, "I have great hope
      in God." This will inspire your spirit
      and lift your mood.
3. Always remind yourself that God's eyes are
    watching over you in everything you do in
    your life.
    - This will bring to you a feeling of
      security.
    - Also, you will try to do the right thing
      no matter what.
4. Always know that God has numbered every
    single hair on your head, and that none of
    them will fall without His permission (Luke
    12:7).
    - He has absolute, immeasurable
      accuracy.
5. Always know that God chooses the best for
    you.
    - What we choose for ourselves is
      what we think is good, but what God
      chooses for us is always the best.

6. Always know that God will put you in the right place and the right time according to His plans.

7. Always be thankful for the little things, and those little things will turn into bigger things.

8. Always do what God wants you to do.
   - He will equip you to do so.
   - Inner peace and family consensus is a sign to proceed.

9. Always talk about the positive.
   - Talking about the positives will make us focus our energy on them.
   - Focusing our energy will make us excel in our work.

10. Always read carefully when you work and study.
    - Don't just skim; you may miss something very important.
    - Getting into this habit makes you pay attention to details that may be important.

11. Always try to recognize the Adversary's voice:
    - It gives you false security.
    - It makes you count your material possessions.
    - Sometimes it says, "Nobody is as good as you."
    - Sometimes it says, "What will happen? Just do it."

- When you hear the Adversary's voice, say, "Lord have mercy on me."

12. Always listen to your spouse when he/she is talking.
    - The act of listening is a source of joy to your spouse.
    - He/she is your partner in your blissful life.

13. Always be assertive with your manager when he calls you to work for him on your day off.
    - Especially when you have family plans already (your son's soccer game, your daughter's dance recital).

14. Always respect the wishes of your spouse.
    - Ignorance is the primary tool that is used by the Adversary to break up wonderful relationships.
    - This respect for your spouse's wishes is a part of love.

15. Always love all people because they are the creation of God.
    - Loving them is a part of your love for God.
    - Make sure that you ignore the "bad" in people.

16. Always keep your eyes focused on the Author of Life and you will have ultimate guidance in your life.

17. Always have peace with God, and your peace will be abundant and never-ending.

18. Always have peace with yourself.

- Because God is in you.
- If peace is in you, peace will be all around you.

19. Always know what the purpose of your life is and how to fulfill this purpose.

20. Always do what you know is the right thing—not to gain commendation from people but because you have goodness inside you.

21. Always react positively to life, no matter how bad the reality is, until life responds back in a positive way.
    - You can change the negatives in your life by reacting positively.
    - Then life will change and these negatives will be just history in your memory that you will laugh about one day.

22. Always be aware of the verbal and non-verbal keys of communication.
    - Be mindful of your facial expressions; they say a lot.

23. Always know your capabilities, what you can do and what you cannot do.
    - If you do what you can, you will succeed in it.
    - Don't start something that you cannot finish.

24. Always eat healthy foods.
    - Health is priceless.

25. Always bless God in the morning; He gave you this morning.

- He sends an abundance of blessings to Earth every morning.
- Start with Psalm 103 and observe the magnificent things that will happen to you.

26. Always be prepared for various situations so that you may know how to answer everyone properly.
    - Your spouse: "I had an accident with the car."
    You: "Are you okay? You are important."
    - Someone: "I challenge you."
    You: "Life is a challenge; let us help each other to meet life's challenges head-on."
    - Someone: "You hurt my feelings."
    You: "I am sorry; forgive me; I did not mean to do so."
    - You can add to this list as you go.

27. Always count your blessings—write them in your personal journal and have them handy.
    - This list will be a great asset when temptations come along.
    - Knowing your blessings will be a great source of thankfulness.
    - This list will allow you to see what you have to be thankful for and to not dwell on what is missing. When what is missing comes, you can then add it to your list. Then you find yourself

in an endless cycle of blessings and thankfulness.

28. Always recite your favorite psalm, one that brings peace to your soul in a time of agony.
    - If you do not know one, check out Psalms 16, 20, 23, 34, 91, 121, and 146.

29. Always choose carefully what you watch on TV.
    - Your mind is not a trash can.
    - You may watch something that may, unintentionally, affect your behavior.

30. Always be in a position of peace.
    - God is at peace at all times.
    - Since you are connected to God, you should be at peace at all times as well.
    - When you are in the position of peace, you are in the position of power.
    - You always want to be in the position of power.

31. Always be humble.
    - Pride destroyed angels.
    - Arrogance destroyed great historical figures.

32. Always control your thoughts, so that you can control your life.

33. Always choose the right time to do the right things.
    - There is a time for everything.

34. Always choose the most appropriate way to express your thoughts.
     - As much it matters what you say, it also matters how you say it.
35. Always ask God for guidance in all of the aspects of your life.
     - For He said, "Counsel is mine, and sound wisdom" (Proverbs 8:14).
     - When you do so, "He will instruct you the way you should go" (Psalm 32:8).
     - When you know what you have to do, you can say, "I can do all things through Christ who strengthens me" (Philippians 4:13).
36. Always read and take heed.
     - A man can write his seventy-year life experience in a book that you can read in seven days. How awesome is this?
     - Then apply what wisdom you have read into your life.
     - Doing this will add knowledge to your experience. Then you take heed from this life experience.
     - Always remember that reading is a source of light to a man's mind.
37. Always recall these facts:
     - Anyone can be deceived by the Adversary at any time about anything, you and me included.
     - None of us is immune.

- God's wisdom and our humbleness keep us safe from these traps.
38. Always pursue true nobility.
    - That is, you become better than what you were before.
39. Always have a collection of favorite scriptures handy on your desk.
    - This will be a great help in a time of challenge.
    - These words will give healing to the soul.
40. Always set goals for each year of your life.
    - For example, "This year I will learn how to practice faithfulness."
    - Soon you will have all the fruits of the Spirit.
41. Always make a map of your life.
    - Determine your goals clearly.
    - These goals must be according to God's will and your own ability.
42. Always be patient.
    - Practice patience until it becomes second nature.
    - Patience has its rewards.
43. Always be impartial.
    - Do not let bias make any part in your decisions.
44. Always exercise your talents.
    - Talents are seeds given to us by God to be planted and bring forth fruit.
    - No one is without talents.

- Know yours; nourish them so that you have fruit in your life.

45. Always sit with yourself on a regular basis.
    - The more you sit with yourself, the more you observe yourself.
    - The more you observe yourself, the more you know about yourself.
    - And when you know yourself, you can improve yourself.

46. Always value every job, no matter how easy it is.
    - If the trash man does not come for two weeks, the house will stink.
    - Do not belittle anyone.

47. Always know that changing behavior and character require time and effort.
    - First, you must be aware of what you want to change.
    - Then you must know what new behavior you want to adopt.
    - Then you must figure out how to get there.

48. Always trim those negative self-destructive thoughts.
    - After pulling them up by their roots, plant new constructive ones.

49. Always explain your feelings, if someone hurt your feelings.
    - But do so without hurting the other person's feelings.
    - Be the peacemaker.

> - This is another way to show true nobility.

50. Always call your supervisor when you are running late.
51. Always give respect to earn respect.
52. Always be sure the salt shaker cap is screwed on tightly so that only a little salt comes out when you use it.

> - Especially when you are cooking for your family.

53. Always think about what God says about you to His angels.
54. Always start with the words "baby," "my love," or "my dear" when you start a conversation with your spouse.

> - Especially if you expect this conversation will bring disagreement.

55. Always learn to resist the temptations and the external forces of the Adversary through the Lord Jesus Christ.
56. Always be meek in your thoughts and meekness will be the nature of your behavior.
57. Always be relaxed, for God is always in complete control.
58. Always make your statements simple, perfect, professional, and concise.
59. Always bless a child and his Creator, God, when you look at a child's smile.
60. Always be sure that when you buy a toy for your child, it has a volume control.

- You may need it when you want some quiet time.
61. Always avoid laziness when you wake up early for church.
    - You never know whether you may hear a message of grace that day that will change your life.
62. Always know that some prayers will not be answered the way you want them to be.
    - They may be right in your eyes, but may not be according to His will.
    - Not all prayers are according to His will and goodness.
63. Always base your behavior on the Bible.
64. Always release the anger from the subconscious.
    - You may not feel it, but it will drive your behavior.
65. Always have a dream and pursue it.
    - First, make sure that the dream is from God.
    - A man with a dream is the one who will rise and give glory to Him.
66. Always keep a balance of different activities in your life.
    - Balance your care for your body, spirit, and mind.
    - Know this: The life of the human spirit is God and His word; the life of the human body is healthy food and

exercise; the life of the human mind is education and pure knowledge.

67. Always know the right way to take care of your body.
    - Protect your body from undue mistakes.
    - Some people get plastic surgery that ends in permanent deformity.

68. Always manage entertaining your son when your spouse gives him to you.
    - Especially if your spouse has been taking care of him all day long.
    - Resist the thought to give him back with the misconception he/she can handle him better.
    - Giving your spouse a break and time for him/herself is one facet of love.

69. Always value your time.
    - You cannot store nor retrieve time.
    - If you know the value of your time, you know the value of your life.
    - If you know the value of your life, you will reach your destiny.

70. Always inspire yourself when you lack motivation.
    - No one will motivate you as much as you can yourself.

71. Always focus on the wonderful things in your life.

72. Always call your family members and close friends during the morning of their birthday.
    - Doing this will make them feel special and give them a positive start to their day.
    - If you wait until evening, you may forget.
73. Always force yourself to walk righteously before God—fasting, praying, and following His commandments.
    - It may be hard at the beginning, but later it will be a natural essence to walk blameless before God.
    - It will take some effort to overcome the inner resistance and external distraction.
    - He will reward by sending angels to keep you safe.
    - You will be sure of your eternity.
74. Always buy Christmas decorations after Christmas is over.
    - Store them for next Christmas.
    - You will get the best deals with very economical prices.
75. Always know how to cook one simple meal, even if you do not like to cook.
    - It will be the most delicious meal when you and your spouse are tired of eating out and bored with pizza.

76. Always taste your friends' food in restaurants.
    - Next time you go out to eat, you'll have different options based on real experience.
77. Always take your cell phone out of your pocket before getting into the car.
    - Your seat belt will be a great obstacle if you are driving and the phone goes off.
78. Always turn off your cell phone in church.
    - God is more important than any call.
    - You want your prayers to be answered.
    - You don't want to disturb others who are praying around you.
79. Always consider the following facts when you are thinking of marriage:
    - Look for a good spirit, high morals, wisdom, and fear of God.
        - ☐ These no one can steal.
        - ☐ These are pillars of a successful marriage.
    - Do not go for looks; they can deceive and can fade away.
    - Do not go for wealth; even that fades away.
    - Go for someone who makes your heart smile; a smile makes your life bright.

80. Always show empathy to a man who talks to you about his agony.
   - You just offered him a priceless thing: a listening ear and a caring heart.
   - Expressing his feelings to someone who cares gives him relief.
81. Always determine and pursue good character.
   - Have fervent faith and a positive attitude.
   - Be quiet and confident.
   - Weigh your words and speak in a low tone of voice.
   - Be thoughtful and use self-control.
82. Always improve your listening skills.
   - Allow the speaker to finish talking.
   - Hearing is not always listening; listening involves comprehension of what was said.
   - Remember St. James's advice: "Let every man be swift to hear, slow to speak, slow to wrath" (1:19).
83. Always remember these verses and control your tongue:
   - "In the multitude of words sin is not lacking, but he who restrains his lips is wise" (Proverbs 10:19).
   - When you speak: "Let your speech always be with grace, seasoned with salt, that you may know how

you ought to answer each one"
(Colossians 4:6).

84. Always act from a heart full of God.
- If you act from a heart full of God,
you will never make mistakes.
- If you would like to fill your heart
with God, keep His commandments.

85. Always remember who you want to be and
how you can get there.
- Fulfillment of your destiny brings
magnificent joy.

86. Always remember that everything depends
on your way of thinking; everything is a
decision.
- Think positively and decide to be
happy and wise.

87. Always know that wherever you are,
wherever you go, God will be there.
- He is omnipresent.

88. Always keep your mind occupied with
the word of God and you will win every
challenge in life.

89. Always expect God's help, and don't be
afraid to ask for it.
- The more you expect God's help, the
more you receive God's help.

90. Always look at the Master of the universe,
and walk according to His word, even if your
future seems vague to you.
- Little by little, He will unfold
vagueness and make your life bright.

91. Always remember these verses—the secret to happiness is in them:
- "No one, having put his hand to the plow, and looking back, is fit for the kingdom of God" (Luke 9:62), so do not look at the past.
- "Therefore do not worry about tomorrow, for tomorrow will worry about its own things" (Matthew 6:34), so do not fear tomorrow.
- "This is the day the Lord has made; we will rejoice and be glad in it" (Psalm 118:24), so be happy today.

92. Always adjust your speed to God's speed.
- If you let go of His hand and run, you may fall, and you will fall behind.

93. Always gain an assertive personality.
- Know your rights.
- Know your duties.
- Have a realistic view on matters of life.
- Make the proper decision in the right time.

94. Always know that your thoughts are revealed in front of God.
- Nothing can hinder God's eyes.
- It is your decision to accept or resist any thought.
- With all your power, resist any bad thought.

- Why let a bad thought become an obstacle between you and God?

95. Always know that God will not permit you a trial in your life unless you can bear it.
   - Remember: "God is faithful, who will not allow you to be tempted beyond what you are able, but with the temptation will also make the way of escape, that you may be able to bear it" (1 Corinthians 10:13).

96. Always slow down that inner dialogue that takes a great deal of your concentration every day.

97. Always do the natural part, and God will do the supernatural part.
   - He will not do anything independently of you; you have to do your part.

98. Always determine your weaknesses and make them the subject of your prayer.

99. Always complain only to the One who can help, God.
   - Remember the woman of Shunem (2 Kings 4:8), who complained only to the prophet, who represented God?
   - She neither complained to her husband nor to the prophet's assistant.
   - Then God will send you someone who truly can help you.

100. Always be the master of your mind.

- You can choose your thoughts.
- Feelings follow thoughts.
- Thus, you can choose your feelings.

101. Always determine the amount of time that you will spend in front of the TV.
    - The more time you spend in front of TV, the less time you spend with yourself.

102. Always know that the Adversary will attack when you are tired and exhausted.
    - Recognize yourself when you are subject to this vulnerability.
    - Draw back from communication when you are vulnerable.
    - Regenerate your energy.

103. Always be sure to have true godly peace before you pursue anything.
    - Make this request in your prayer: "According Your will, O Lord, fill my heart with Your peace."
    - This will keep you safe from false peace.

104. Always know that there is one life and one death.
    - The only thing we can carry with us is what we did for Jesus and His brethren.
    - Remember: "Inasmuch as you did it to one of the least of these My brethren, you did it to Me" (Matthew 25:40).

105. Always remember that you are made in God's image and your spirit is part of His Spirit (Genesis 1:26; 2:7).
    - Make your spirit strong; connect it to Him (1 Corinthians 6:17).
106. Always know that a bright future is the son of a beautiful dream in the present that you pursued and achieved.
107. Always know that every divine promise has its conditions.
    - Fulfill these conditions, and you will receive the promise.
    - We have unanswered prayers because we do not fulfill the divine conditions.
108. Always know that it is a terrible thing to live in fear.
    - Sin is the worst fear.
    - Before you sin, ask yourself, "Am I able to live in fear?"
109. Always value your family.
    - If you have to choose between your family and a promotion with relocation, choose family.
    - Promotions can come and go, but not family.
    - Never be deceived by the Adversary, who can make you say, "I am doing this for the family."
110. Always know that love is a source of joy when it is right.

- Lust is a source of pain and it is not right.
- Never get confused between these two L-words.

111. Always calibrate your standards to God's.
     - Having blue glasses on will make everything look blue even though things may actually be white or green.

112. Always strengthen your will.
     - Repeat statements that will make your will strong, such as: "I can do all things through Christ who strengthens me" (Philippians 4:13).
     - Then, when you have a strong will, achievement and success will be easy goals for you.

113. Always meditate on the power of God.
     - You will bring the power of God into your life.
     - Every one of us needs the power of God in his life.

114. Always forgive others (and yourself).
     - What you forgive, you must forget and never bring up again; otherwise, you never really forgave.
     - Forgiving will give you a pure and peaceful mind.
     - It is the Lord's command that we forgive.

115. Always hope for good things to happen in your life, and they will happen.

116. Always depend on the power of fervent prayer to solve any problem, great or small.
     - If you do not know the power of prayer in this wild world, you are like a soldier without a weapon in a tough war.
     - If you do not know a prayer, ask Him how to pray to Him. He will guide you.
117. Always listen with a grain of salt.
     - Do not believe all that is said.
     - This is one of the differences between a wise and foolish man.
118. Always pray in the name of the Lord Jesus Christ.
     - This name holds a great power.
     - All of us need power.
     - Remember what St. Paul said: "Whatever you do in word or deed, do all in the name of the Lord Jesus" (Colossians 3:17).
119. Always use a calendar or a planner to organize the matters of your life.
     - You do not want to forget what you want to remember.
120. Always respond to people's bad behavior with goodness.
     - Your reaction will be unexpected.
     - This will cut the endless cycle of hatred, anger, and anxiety.
     - There is goodness inside you, but the challenge is to use it in these situations.

121. Always treat your spouse with the same love and affection that you did at the beginning of your relationship.
122. Always be generous with genuine compliments, and stingy with criticisms.
    - Words cost you nothing.
    - Inspiring words are the windows to a merry heart.
123. Always run to the Lord when you are troubled and in agony.
    - Christ says, "Come to Me, all you who labor and are heavy laden, and I will give you rest" (Matthew 11:28).
    - Those who are still in agony have not yet gone to Him.
124. Always be careful in the present.
    - If mistakes of the past influence the present, try to not make mistakes in the present so you do not waste the future.
    - Know that thinking of and regretting mistakes of the past is just adding another mistake to the past.
125. Always resist negative thoughts, especially those that come at bedtime.
126. Always accept yourself and love yourself.
    - Always do your best to improve yourself.
127. Always know that your grades are proportional to your study effort and skills.

- The more you study, the better grades
you get.
128. Always know that success is the result of hard
work.
- Luck has no share in success.
- If you study hard, you will succeed no
matter how unlucky you feel.
129. Always know these facts:
- You can change your world by
changing your words.
- You can change your words by
changing your thoughts.
- You can change your thoughts by
letting God live in your mind.
130. Always know that a marriage will only
succeed when there is a completion and not
competition.
- Respect and honesty are two
absolutely necessary pillars for a
successful marriage.
131. Always know that a child means life, and life
is the result of love.
- Abortion means death, and death is
the result of lust.
132. Always know that divorce is the result of
hatred and hardness of heart.
- Where is that tender heart that you
started with? Where is that love?
- Look for it and bring it back.
133. Always build your decisions on facts and not
opinions.

134. Always know that your mental attitude toward circumstances, not the circumstances themselves, causes you happiness or misery.
     - If the reality is bad, what is your reaction to it?
     - Is it positive or negative?
     - When you change your mental attitude towards circumstances, these circumstances will change.
135. Always stop the feeling of being right, better, or superior to others.
     - These are ego delusions.
     - We're all just branches in one tree called humanity.
136. Always take your time doing things right from the beginning.
     - Haste makes waste.
     - Shame is a burden.
     - Regrets will profit you nothing.
137. Always say, "God please bless my time."
     - But never say, "I do not have the time," especially when it comes to your family or goals.
     - If you need time, you must create it.
138. Always control your senses, and it will be easy to control your thoughts.
     - Wild senses lead to a restless mind.
139. Always care for His commandments.
     - He will take care of everything in your life.

- Isn't it nice to just take care of the little things and leave the rest to Him?

140. Always know that problems exist when you do not have contact with God.
    - When the Adversary puts a dark sheet over your eyes, remove it.

141. Always learn from your mistakes and the mistakes of others.
    - Doing so will make you live life with fewer mistakes.

142. Always know the objective of what you are doing.
    - Objectives make priorities.
    - Time spent with no objectives is discouraging.
    - Having no clear objectives makes life absurd.
    - Having clear objectives makes life meaningful.

143. Always apologize when you do or say something wrong.
    - It is a sign of a strong personality.
    - It is a sign of a humble heart.
    - It prevents conflict.

144. Always stay in good physical shape.
    - If you cannot afford going to the gym, walk around the block.
    - Instead of eating junk food, cook healthy food.

145. Always think objectively and with a sense of purpose.
    - If you do not know how, learn how.
146. Always be on time for everything (even the little things).
    - It shows you respect others' time.
147. Always expect to meet the right people in your life, and then you will attract them into your life.
148. Always watch your ego.
    - It can become a huge obstacle to good relationships and achievement.
149. Always fear the One.
    - That is, God.
    - You will not then fear anything else because who is bigger than God?
    - And when you fear God, His angels will be around you keeping you safe (Psalm 34).
150. Always know the right and appropriate way to reach your goals.
    - There is always a way when there is a will.
151. Always have your ears sensitive to God's voice.
    - Listen to that quiet, soft voice in your heart
    - It is the voice of God.
    - But never follow that harsh loud voice; it is the voice of the Adversary.

152. Always pursue higher spiritual awareness.
    - When you reach a high level of spiritual awareness, you will discover the divine resources within you.
    - When you discover the divine resources within you, you will find that you are complete and unique, and you will encounter magnificent things in your life.
    - Then just observe and praise God.
153. Always know that the happiest people do not have the best of everything; they just make the most of everything they have.
    - Learn to make the most of your life and you make your happiness by yourself.
    - Always wanting what you do not have is not always right.
154. Always know that there is a great unseen wisdom of God behind everything that happens in your life.
    - Even if it looks wrong or absurd to you, it is there.
    - With patience, confidence of His love, and connectedness to Him, you will realize this wisdom.
155. Always know that successful relationships are based on mutual respect and a sense of ethical fairness.
    - These relationships are crowned with fulfillment and joy.

156. Always be optimistic.
    - Especially in the face of challenge.
    - See success as something attainable.
    - Know that the sun shines behind the dark clouds.
    - A sound mind and healthy body greatly depend on hoping for the best.
157. Always create a positive image of yourself and do your best to achieve it.
158. Always know that the mercy of God is bigger than any sin.
    - This includes all sins that a person did, does, or will do.
    - This also includes the sins of the whole world.
159. Always stop the train of your negative thought from the beginning, before it gets faster and you cannot stop it.
160. Always observe your thoughts and pursue the good ones.
    - If you're not sure how to "observe" your thoughts, write them down.
161. Always seek wisdom.
    - Know God to get wisdom: "For the Lord gives wisdom; from His mouth comes knowledge and understanding" (Proverbs 2:6).
    - "Happy is the man who finds wisdom" (Proverbs 3:13).
    - All of us want to be happy; wisdom gives strength to the spirit and brightness to the mind.

- Calmness of mind is one of the
  beautiful fruits of wisdom.
162. Always make a bubble around yourself filled
with positive energy and thoughts.
  - It is your shield against the wild world.
  - The source of this shield is God.
  - Never let anyone penetrate this
    bubble and diffuse your energy.
163. Always know that you are rich.
  - Not with money, but just for the fact
    that you know and believe in the
    Lord Jesus Christ.
164. Always know that no one has everything he
wants.
  - No one can be sure of keeping what
    he has.
165. Always do good, even to those who hurt you.
  - If you are tempted not to, remember
    your sins and that God still provides
    good things to you.
166. Always strive for honesty and perfection at
work, not reputation.
167. Always do your duties before you ask for
your rights.
168. Always secure yourself against stress.
  - Learn and practice how to handle it
    in the right way.
169. Always look at your blind spot before you
switch lanes when driving a car.
  - We forget to do this when we are
    talking on the phone.

- Your safety is a priority.

170. Always surround yourself with a good support system of good friends and wise people so that you know where to turn when the road gets rough.

171. Always ponder mistakes of the past, but do not be trapped in deep regret for them.
    - Consider why you made the mistakes in order to avoid them in the future.
    - You may write it in your diary to help you remember.

172. Always care about the peace of your house with your spouse and your children.
    - Division in a house is a sign that the Adversary has succeeded in his temptation.

173. Always train your child in the right path while he is young, and he will grow up walking on that right path.
    - This will bring you joy and fulfillment.

174. Always teach your child good things that you did not get a chance to learn when you were a child.

175. Always keep the landscaping guy informed about important occasions such as exams and parties
    - You do not want him to come the day before the exam with all these machines and make your lose your concentration.

- You do not want him to come the day that you have a party and annoy your visitors.

176. Always say, "Have a blessed day."
    - The word "blessed" includes all the others—wonderful, great, and nice.

177. Always have some answers prepared when your children ask you tough questions.
    - "The heart of the righteous studies how to answer" (Proverbs 15:28).

178. Always endure to the end.
    - This is the character of winners.

179. Always arrive one hour early for an exam.
    - Relaxation before an exam is one tool of good test-taking.

180. Always come to a job interview half an hour before the interview.
    - You want to impress your potential employer.

181. Always take your medications on time.
    - Your health is important.
    - Ask your pharmacist about tools to help adhere to compliance with taking medication.

182. Always ask your doctor about the goal of your therapy.
    - If you do not know the goal of your therapy, how can you know what you want to achieve?
    - Also, prepare questions for your doctor before the visit; be proactive in your health.

183. Always have your list of medications with you in your wallet/purse.
    - Make sure to include all herbals and supplements.
    - Know that some herbals can interact with medication.
184. Always determine the most productive time of your day and give it the priorities and tasks that require the highest concentration.
185. Always keep a journal.
    - Write down the good things that you learned in school, work, or from a friend.
    - The more you write down of what you have learned and applied in your life, the better quality of life you will have.
186. Always put the camera strap around your neck or your hand when using it.
    - Do this especially when you are taking pictures near water or children.
187. Always put a gallon of water in the trunk of your car.
    - You never know when you will need it.
188. Always put Tums in your office.
    - You may need it when you order a pizza or double burger.
189. Always know what things will refresh your energy and cheer you up.
190. Always know that changes in life must happen.

- Take a positive attitude toward them.
191. Always know that not every expensive car is reliable.
192. Always cover the dashboard of your car with a sunshade especially in summer.
193. Always keep the snow scraper and shovel in your car in winter, especially in northern states.
194. Always be careful with promises before marriage.
    - Things look flowery before marriage.
    - Challenges look impossible after marriage.
    - Don't make promises you may not be able to keep.
195. Always know that one mistake leads to another.
    - Cut the endless cycle of mistakes and fix the first one.
    - Never refuse to correct a mistake.
196. Always listen to your favorite music when you are stressed.
197. Always have at least a small idea about car parts and keep maintenance records of your car.
    - Your honest mechanic may relocate.
198. Always put your car keys, wallet, and cell phone in the same spot in your house.
    - It will be easy to grab all of them in any situation.
    - If anything is missing, it will be easy to figure it out.

199. Always trust street signs vs. your navigation system if they are telling you two different things.
    - Street signs are what is real; the navigation system is second-hand information.
200. Always count your steps to your goals.
    - Never take unnecessary steps that will distract you from your goals.
201. Always rent a trailer and tow your car if you are traveling a great distance to a new home in order to avoid wear and tear on your vehicle.
    - Whatever the cost of the trailer, it will save your car's struts system and high mileage.
202. Always balance your checkbook.
203. Always check your credit card statement against your receipts.
204. Always differentiate for your son the difference between not loving him and not loving his behavior.
    - Let him know that you always love him but that you do not always agree with certain behavior.
205. Always take many photos and then decide which one is good for your album.
206. Always wipe a can of soda's top before you open it.
207. Always hold your wife's hand when it is raining.

- Especially if she is pregnant.
- If you have a baby, please carry the baby.
- Absolutely always hold your wife's hand on a date.

208. Always choose the love of a faithful spouse rather than riches.
    - Never fall into the trap that riches can bring you a good spouse.
    - A faithful partner is priceless; once you find him/her, hold on tight and don't let go.

209. Always make a collection of movies, especially true stories to teach your son the wisdom behind them.

210. Always inspect a house that you are about to buy and match your list with inspector's list.
    - This will save you a lot of surprises if you purchase the house.

211. Always seek knowledge and understanding.
    - A man of knowledge is always needed in his career.

212. Always know that if you eat more than you need, you will retain fat even though the food is fat-free.

213. Always turn off the Bluetooth in your car if you're not using it.
    - If it is on and you are receiving a call, those who are in the car will hear your conversation.

214. Always write your name on gifts. A lot of people get carried away by wrapping the gift, which they forget to put their name on.
215. Always compliment your wife when she wears a new dress and when she changes her hairstyle.
216. Always check the charge of your cell phone before you go to bed.
217. Always chew gum when your flight is taking off and when it is landing.
    - This will decrease the air pressure in your ears.
218. Always have a blank, unsigned check in your wallet.
    - It may be the only way of payment in certain unexpected situations.
219. Always leave a shopping center where there is a traffic light.
    - It is better to be under the mercy of a traffic light than to be under the mercy of ongoing traffic.
220. Always hope for the best but be prepared for the worst.
221. Always say thanks when you sneeze and no one says bless you.
    - Those who did not say it will laugh and say it afterwards.
222. Always have a picture of the Lord Jesus Christ in the middle of your house with a candle or small lamp in front of it with a

sign underneath saying, "Keep Your eyes on this house."

- When you have an unpleasant unexpected letter or news that might shake the peace and the security of your house, put it behind the picture.
- Then start to pray that the Lord will take care of whatever is in that letter.

223. Always put your most often called contacts on speed dial.

224. Always check your flight status before going to the airport.

- If your flight gets delayed when you are in the airport, be prepared with an inspirational book that you bought but never had the chance to read.
- Note that if you make your cell phone your only entertainment device, you may increase your frustration.
- Note that if you keep calling your friends to tell them about your delayed flight, you also increase your frustration.

225. Always remember where you parked your car, especially at an airport, theme park, or hospital.

226. Always keep some type of laundry detergent stick or wipes with you.

- You never know when you'll need it (especially if you have children).

227. Always know that what comes easy will be lost easily.
228. Always worship God without regard for His gifts.
    - Sometimes we receive what we ask for.
    - Other times, God knows better what we need and answers our prayer with, "No."
    - Worship and thank Him regardless of how He answers your prayers.
229. Always stay up-to-date on CPR.
    - You don't know when you might need it.
    - Keep your knowledge about basic life support active.
    - Saving a person's life is priceless.
230. Always keep a plastic bag in your car.
    - Use it to dump unwanted stuff/trash in your car.
    - Your car will stay clean.
231. Always pay your tithe.
    - Watch for the abundance of blessings in every aspect of your life.
    - For more information, please review Malachi 3:10.
232. Always guard the purity and peace of your brain.
    - Your brain is your computer. If it does not function well, your whole body will not function well.
233. Always cast your vote according to what God puts in your heart, and not according to people's persuasion.

- Remember: "The king's heart is in the hand of the Lord, like the rivers of water; He turns it wherever He wishes" (Proverbs 21:1).

234. Always make your signature unique.
    - It is one way to avoid identity theft.

235. Always call your parents when they are retired and need your support.
    - Remember how they supported you when you were younger.

236. Always read the instructions on a bag of fertilizer carefully before using it.
    - Fertilizer can harm your lawn if you misuse it.

237. Always go the extra mile when helping others.
    - Remember with the same measure you use, it will be measured back to you.

238. Always be a friend to your children.
    - Let them come to you at any time, no matter what.

239. Always be prepared for the following day by reviewing your agenda before leaving your office.

240. Always encourage your children to have a summer job according to their age and ability.
    - It does not matter if these jobs are volunteer or paid.
    - By the time they settle in their career, they will know a good amount about life.

241. Always help your children to discover:
    - What talents they have;
    - What they want to be when they grow up;
    - What blessings they have.
242. Always check with your spouse's family about what gift to buy if you are unsure.
    - They may have insight.
243. Always collect quotes and sentences that touch your heart from that nice book that you're reading.
    - Apply them to your life.
    - You may not have enough time to read the entire book again.
    - Keep this collection for your children.
244. Always keep notes for your children about how you and your spouse overcome marital challenges.
    - These notes will come in handy when they face theirs.
245. Always use credit cards with different billing cycles.
    - Make sure billing cycles match the time of your incoming checks.
246. Always remember this biblical rule.
    - "And just as you want men to do to you, you also do to them likewise" (Luke 6:31).
    - Treat others as you would like to be treated.

- Love them as you want to be loved.
- Care for them as you want them to care for you.
- Be the starter of kindness and gentleness.

247. Always apologize to an officer when you get pulled over and you know you broke the traffic rules.
- Never argue with him.
- Be ready with your ID and insurance card.
- This may save you a lot.

248. Always take enough water with your medication.
- It has an important part in the drug's efficacy.

249. Always make sure to spend some time with your family in a park or garden.
- It is good for the human soul to spend time in nature.
- Make memories and take pictures.

250. Always keep the Christmas spirit all year long.
- It is the spirit of generosity, kindness, and love.

Never

1. Never talk about the past, because you cannot change it.
      - Remembering the good times of the past is okay.
      - Talking about the past is wasting the present.
2. Never talk about the negatives in your life or other people's lives; discern these negatives, but do not let the Adversary know about these negatives.
3. Never boast nor talk about your grades.
      - Do not let the Adversary pay attention to your success; then he can tempt you.
4. Never boast about your career.
5. Never boast about your promotion or rewards.
6. Never boast about your weight loss in front of someone struggling to lose weight.
      - However, you can let them know how you did it if they ask.
      - Encourage in a positive way.
7. Never thank God for something that you have in front of someone who does not have that thing.

- Care for the emotions and feelings of others.

8. Never say the word "hate."
   - Instead, use "dislike."

9. Never put yourself down.
   - Even someone with a mental illness will tell you that he is completely sane. If he can say that about himself, why can't you?

10. Never say, "This is wrong."
    - Instead, say, "It does not seem right for me," but remember that something not right for you may be right for others.

11. Never call someone "stupid" for something they did.
    - Instead, say, "That wasn't a smart decision."

12. Never call someone a liar.
    - This is a very harsh word to say.
    - Instead, say that he is not telling the truth.
    - Next time be very careful dealing with this person.

13. Never say, "What the hell?" or "What the heck?"
    - These are harsh to the ears; they give a bad impression to listeners.
    - Instead, just say, "What is this?"

14. Never say, "You do not have what it takes to succeed."

- If a person has God, he/she has everything needed to succeed.

15. Never remind a man of his weaknesses, his bad deeds or mistakes, or bad days in his life.
    - This is unwise behavior.
    - Every man would like to forget these things.
    - Do not cause him more pain by reminding him of these things.

16. Never put yourself in a conflict with anyone.
    - Be assertive about your rights.
    - Defuse situations.
    - It is great wisdom to be in peace with everyone.
    - You may need that person tomorrow; no one knows what the future holds.

17. Never announce your weaknesses.
    - Do not say, "This pisses me off."
        - Saying that will make the Adversary know which button to push to stress you out.
        - Just ignore it.

18. Never show your panic.
    - Even if you are terrified on the inside, just stay calm.
    - Remember these two promises:
        - "Fear not for I am with you" (Isaiah 41:10).
        - "In quietness and confidence is your strength" (Isaiah 30:15).

19. Never say what you may regret later.
    - Remember that words last longer than a man's age. Those who hear your words will still remember them after you pass away.
    - Words that come out of your mouth are not yours alone anymore.
20. Never let a day pass without thanking God.
    - He gives you that day to proceed and succeed in life.
    - Doing so will let you see His blessings in that day.
21. Never lose hope in God; He is the king of hope.
22. Never lose hope in yourself.
    - If God does not lose hope in you, why do you lose hope in yourself?
23. Never point out the material possessions of anyone.
    - Most people infer that you are envying them when you do so.
24. Never compare yourself to someone else.
    - Insist on being yourself.
    - You are unique.
    - When you have a positive image of yourself, you will discover how you are unique.
25. Never do something in secret that in public you would be ashamed of.
26. Never say, "I promise."
    - Instead, say, "God willing."

- Shame comes when we promise and we do not fulfill.

27. Never forget to buy gifts for special occasions.
    - Anniversaries.
    - Birthdays of your spouse, parents, children.
    - Christmas.
    - Father's Day.
    - Mother's Day.
    - Valentine's Day.

28. Never allow hatred into your heart.
    - One day, it will be revealed.
    - One day it will hurt you.
    - Why carry negative things inside? Let them go.

29. Never say a bad word about anyone.
    - As you say about others, others say about you.
    - You do not want others to say anything bad about you, so don't say anything bad about them.

30. Never let a mistake make you lose confidence in yourself.
    - Instead, learn from it, fix it, and boost your confidence in yourself.

31. Never do something that you and your spouse do not agree on.
    - Consensus is a sign of safety and success.

32. Never abuse your energy.

- Your body will hurt you badly.
- Energy is needed all the time; if you abuse it, you will lose it.
- Give your body the rest that it needs.

33. Never say a word that you do not mean.
    - A genuine man is always trusted.
    - Why lose people's trust?

34. Never say something you are not sure about.
    - This will affect your credibility with people.

35. Never run after money to become rich thinking this is ambition.
    - Switching jobs frequently and chasing promotions are signs of this.
    - Knowing what you have is enough will be enough. You can adjust your lifestyle to make it enough.
    - Remember: "The blessing of the Lord makes one rich, and He adds no sorrow with it" (Proverbs 10:22).

36. Never say, "This will not/cannot/does not happen to me."
    - The Adversary may tempt you with the same thing.

37. Never boast about the future.
    - You do not know what the future holds.
    - Just be optimistic.

38. Never think that God is not listening.
    - This is one of the Adversary's deceptions.

- Wait for God's time.

39. Never drive behind a garbage truck.
    - If you have to do so, be sure the "recycle air" button is on in your car.

40. Never say to your spouse "I hate you," "I'm sick of you," or "I regret the day that I married you" in moments of anger.
    - You just deeply injure yourself and your spouse.
    - This hurts forever.
    - Hundreds of romantic nights will not take this from his or her subconscious.
    - Instead, learn how to get over the anger and marriage challenges.

41. Never take medications without reading your medication label first.
    - Those who are wearing white coats are human and can make mistakes.

42. Never do something that will hurt your relationship with God.
    - If you do, the same Adversary who helped you to hurt this relationship will make you imagine that God is against you.
    - Then you will feel insecure because you have lost this sacred rapport and will be slow to repent and confess your sin.
    - Watch for this pitfall.

43. Never ignore the Bible's standards.

- That is where trouble begins.
44. Never let your youth go without finishing your education.
   - Do not waste the years of your youth.
   - Use the strength of your youth to secure your life by getting a good education.
45. Never let adulthood come on you without establishing your career.
46. Never let old age come on you without a plan for retirement.
47. Never correct your boss in front of others.
   - Gently point out the mistake between the two of you.
   - Comment on the behavior not the person.
48. Never put a white napkin on black pants.
   - When you go to a restaurant, ask for black napkin if you are wearing dark pants.
   - White lint from the white napkin will stick to your black pants.
49. Never do an action that you know will bring on a reaction that you do not like.
   - If you expect that you will not like the reaction, do not do the action.
50. Never ask a frugal man for help.
   - You will just humiliate yourself.
51. Never close your door to your son who has just left the house.
   - If you want to know what to do, read Luke 15.

52. Never let the Adversary steal your joy.
    - It is his intention to do so, but it is your duty to protect your joy.
53. Never resist an ice cream sundae on a Sunday evening with your family.
    - It will be great refreshment for the following week.
54. Never forget the map of your life, where you are, and where you are going.
    - You may end up somewhere that you do not like.
55. Never oppress a man because you are stronger.
    - One day, one who is stronger than you will oppress you.
    - What goes around comes around.
    - If you think that you are immune, you are mistaken.
56. Never let a dusty book cover fool you.
    - You might find great wisdom in that book.
    - Take wisdom regardless of where it is found.
57. Never overdo rewarding yourself.
    - Little by little, rewarding will become spoiling.
    - Then one day your soul will be like a wild horse that you cannot capture.
58. Never let money control your rules and standards.
    - It is good to make money, but never let money make your standards.

- Money will not always be there.

59. Never base your happiness on your circumstances.

   - Happiness comes from inside.

60. Never forget to clean your brain from futile thoughts so that good ones can grow and prosper.

   - It is good to do so on regular basis.

61. Never reveal what happens in your house to strangers.

   - What happen in the house stays in the house.
   - Abuse is an exception to that rule.

62. Never compare your family to your spouse's family.

   - No two families are exactly the same.
   - No one family is better than the other; they're just different.

63. Never go shopping without the list on the refrigerator.

64. Never make a decision when you are stressed and have disturbed emotions.

   - Negative emotions can bring about wrong decisions.
   - Wait until you have a serene mind.

65. Never compromise your morals.

   - Your conscience will hurt you badly.
   - Healing of this act may take some time.

66. Never carry out every thought or idea that comes to your mind.

- Test it first; is it from God or the Adversary?
- One thought can lead to an undo mistake.
- If the Adversary pushes you one time, he will push all the time.
- Have mercy on yourself and test your thoughts first.

67. Never regret what you did.
    - You cannot change the past.
    - Learn from your mistakes and move on.
    - Instead of regretting, look how to correct what you did.

68. Never let your son make the same mistake that you did.
    - It is your job to warn him.

69. Never order "extra cheese" in restaurants.
    - You will have to go to the gym to burn the extra calories.
    - You will have to take pills to lower your cholesterol.

70. Never stand behind the door in a public place.
    - Those who are entering do not know that you are there.
    - This happens frequently when we dry our hands in a public restroom.

71. Never start to study for an exam the night before that exam.

- The Adversary will play his role in making you panic.
- Also, it can be difficult to grasp all the material in one night.

72. Never say that an exam is easy.
- It may look easy, but it is not (looks can be deceiving).
- This can make you lose your vigilance and then make mistakes.
- Then it is embarrassing that you made mistakes on an easy exam.

73. Never say that an exam is hard.
- Instead, say, "If others can do it, so can I."
- It is just an exam, which will soon pass, among many in life.
- Do your best to get it over with.

74. Never forget your friend who stood by you in hard circumstances.
- This is a very strong friendship.
- Christmas cards or phone calls will keep the communication going.

75. Never open your car door too wide.
- You will hit the other car in your garage or parking lot.
- If every one of us learns this rule, our cars wouldn't have so many scratches.

76. Never commend (or brag about) yourself.
- Let others do that.
- Give glory to God.

- People infer this as an ego; you do
  not want anyone to misunderstand
  you.
77. Never watch who is passing by.
     - It may be a woman.
     - Others may notice and infer you are
       watching her.
78. Never quit improving yourself.
     - It is a long journey and it starts by
       knowing yourself.
     - Nothing's better than becoming the
       master of yourself.
79. Never be deceived into thinking that you
    cannot change your behavior.
     - Look at winners and survivors and
       learn from them.
     - Failure will not hurt but will bring
       you closer to success, but losing hope
       will truly hurt.
80. Never communicate with the world when
    you are tired or stressed.
     - The world will communicate back in
       a negative way.
     - Stay silent until you revive your
       energy.
81. Never take the opinion of an unwise man.
     - Unwise behavior will be the result.
82. Never assume.
     - Wrong assumptions lead to wrong
       conclusions.
     - Asking is better than assuming.

83. Never do something against God's will.
    - You may regret this for the rest of your life.
    - Inner peace is the right tool to know God's will.
    - If you don't have this inner peace, do not proceed.
84. Never wash your car when rain is in the forecast.
    - You'll just waste time, energy, and money.
    - Wait for the free carwash (rain) and thank God.
85. Never panic when it's raining hard and you are driving.
    - God has counted each rain drop.
    - Your Creator is watching over you.
86. Never let any man's words change your mood.
    - You are strong from the inside.
    - Maybe this man is deceived by the Adversary to influence your mood.
87. Never let a disagreement become a quarrel.
    - You cannot gather spilled water; in the same way, you cannot erase negative memories.
88. Never forget to secure the lid of your hot coffee.
    - Even if someone will pay compensation, no one will take the pain away.

89. Never wait until the last minute to pack before vacation.
     - You want to be relaxed before vacation.
     - Pack ahead of time.
     - When you start with relaxation, you will enjoy your vacation.
     - When you start with stress, you will not enjoy your vacation as much.
90. Never pretend to be someone you're not.
     - One day, everyone will know.
     - What a burden to carry around, wondering if or when someone will find out.
     - Just be yourself.
       □ If you do not like yourself, improve yourself.
91. Never send an email or letter without proofreading it.
     - This one step may save you a great deal of embarrassment.
92. Never send an email or letter when you are agitated.
     - It will bring agitation.
     - Wait until you calm down.
93. Never think you are the only one who has pain in his life.
     - Remember those who are in hospitals, doctor offices, courts.
     - Do not fall into this negative thought.
94. Never hold your tears when saying goodbye.

- You will feel better afterwards.
- It is human nature.
- It is a sign of an empathetic heart.

95. Never ask a favor from a man who you do not know very well.

96. Never accompany a man who lacks integrity and honesty.
   - You may like his path and lose your morals.
   - Remember bad company leads to corruption.

97. Never be offended if someone does not reply to your phone call or email.
   - Give him the benefit of the doubt.

98. Never ignore the phone calls or emails from anyone, especially those who have offended you.
   - They may want forgiveness.
   - If you ignore the person, you lose the chance for reconciliation.

99. Never tell your son this is right or this is wrong without explaining why.
   - Including the consequences of his action.

100. Never think of yourself as defeated.
   - Think of yourself as a winner instead, and you will be.
   - It is one of the traps of the Adversary, so do not fall there.

101. Never say, "I cannot achieve this."
   - If this achievement is according to God's will and your own ability, you will reach it.

- You will succeed, because He wants success for you, but you have to want it for yourself first.

102. Never despise the poor.
- He has created the poor to test our love.
- Your generosity for the poor is one way to win a better place in Heaven.

103. Never do something if you're not 100% sure you can do it.
- Practice until you are confident.

104. Never say your child was an accident.
- No traffic or cars were involved.
- It may be true that you did not plan for that child, but the divine purpose permitted this spirit to come into our world.
- Nothing God does is a mistake.

105. Never value a man by his clothes.
- Great people are hidden in modest clothes.
- Again, looks can be deceiving.
- If the great inventors of the past came to our day, their clothes would be humble, but they gave us this great technology we are enjoying today.

106. Never ask God to make you better than anyone else who does your job.
- However, ask God to empower you to do your job the best you can according to His standards.

107. Never get offended when a prayer is not answered right away.
     - The absolute divine wisdom has perfect timing.
     - There are many prayers in front of God; give Him time.
108. Never drink too much water before an exam.
     - You will need to go to the restroom, but you cannot.
     - This will take away your concentration.
109. Never leave a question unanswered on an exam.
     - Most answers are hidden in the question.
     - Increase your chances of success by answering all questions.
     - Mark whatever seems right; good surprises can happen.
110. Never let anything shake your trust in God.
111. Never enter a relationship in which you are not sure about your emotions or what the relationship is based on.
     - Heartache can happen.
     - You do not want to add pain into your life.
112. Never argue with a man who thinks he is always right.
     - You will never win.
     - Your silence in front of that man will be considered great wisdom.

113. Never let anything make you doubt God's love for you.
114. Never say there is no love in this world.
    - His abundant love is enough.
    - Do your best to feel and recognize this love, and then the words "no love" will be deleted from your vocabulary.
115. Never spoil your son.
    - Reward him.
    - Spoiled and soft hands hardly succeed.
116. Never tell your son, "You are a bad boy."
    - If this statement comes across his ears, it may stay there forever.
    - Instead say, "Your behavior is not good."
    - Comment on the behavior and not on the person.
    - He is a good boy simply because he is your son.
117. Never start a project without finishing it.
    - Achieved goals are pleasant for the heart.
118. Never argue with your spouse when he or she is exhausted.
    - Recognize the signs of exhaustion.
    - Let him or her cool down.
    - When a person is exhausted, unintentional words come out that may hurt forever.

- Avoid these conversations, especially after coming home from work.

119. Never take on the responsibility of making a loved one feel better when he is having a challenge.
    - The best you can do is to pray for him and provide helpful resources for the situation.
    - The least you can do is to never lose hope.
    - Every challenge happens for a reason; he must decide to overcome the challenge.
    - It is not your responsibility to overcome the challenge for him.
    - If he does not overcome the challenge, you may feel disappointed.

120. Never say any material is too hard to study.
    - You will start to believe your words, and it will seem hard for you.
    - Instead, understand that it is new material; it will just take time.
    - It seems hard because you do not know it; once you know it, it is not hard anymore.

121. Never underestimate the power of your words and your actions.
    - Every single word carries power and brings certain emotions into the listener's heart.
    - Every single action has a reaction.

122. Never forget your camera when you are going on a trip.
    - Also take extra batteries with you.
123. Never take a picture of a man without his permission.
124. Never let your toddler play with your car keys.
    - You may not find them the following morning; you have to go to work, and he will just smile at you.
    - He may drop them somewhere that is inaccessible to you.
    - You do not want him to put these keys in his mouth.
125. Never get on a highway when you are low on gas.
126. Never speed; there is always a cop behind the trees.
    - It is better to be a few minutes late than to call off the entire day because of a speeding ticket.
127. Never make excuses; success is at hand.
    - But if you wait too long it may leave and not come back.
128. Never say about another woman, "She is pretty," in front of your wife.
    - Your wife is the prettiest woman in your eyes.
129. Never answer the phone when you are frustrated.
    - Try to cool down first.

- However, the meek should not get frustrated because the Holy Spirit dwells in them.

130. Never shake the hand of a woman carrying a baby.
      - You don't want her to drop the baby trying to shake your hand.
      - Shaking the baby's hand is a better greeting in such a situation.

131. Never reveal the bad behavior of another man.
      - Someone else will reveal your behavior as well.

132. Never enter in a conversation that you overhear but are not officially invited to participate in.

133. Never say, "I have a good memory."
      - Do not let the Adversary know that you have this blessing.
      - Try to use it for goodness.
      - Learn new things since you have this talent.

134. Never give your spouse advice or correct him or her when your spouse is bathing your son who may be crying.
      - The child needs all the attention in this slippery situation.
      - Help your spouse first and afterwards gently give the advice.

135. Never let your mind become inactive.
      - The inactive mind is a workshop for the Adversary.

136. Never let the Adversary deceive you and make you wrongly use your authority at work.
    - One day you will leave that job.
    - On the Day of Judgment, you will give an account of every single deed.
137. Never take on the negative emotions of others.
    - Show empathy as a reflection of feelings.
    - Keep serenity of mind, so you can help.
    - Always remember that God is in control.
138. Never get frustrated in traffic.
    - Be ready to turn on that inspirational CD that you always want to hear but never had time to play.
    - Try to avoid routes with heavy traffic if possible.
139. Never hold onto something that will constantly worry you.
    - Instead, turn the problem over to God.
140. Never buy something without knowing the return policy.
141. Never buy something and store it for a while before using it.
    - You may start to use it later and find you do not like it.
    - By that time, the return period is over.

142. Never throw away a receipt until you use the product and you are happy and satisfied with the merchandise.
143. Never go sailing or to the beach without checking the weather first.
144. Never sit beside the window on a long flight.
    - You may need to go to the restroom, and the person next to you may be sleeping.
145. Never look at your watch when you are on a date.
146. Never talk about the failure of previous relationships with your new date.
    - Do not bring the mess of the past to the present.
    - Remember that the future is full of new and good surprises.
    - The experience of the past will make you value the right relationship.
147. Never put a phone in your bedroom.
    - You want to sleep, don't you?
    - If you must, make sure you turn the volume down while sleeping.
148. Never let the past determine your future.
    - Use the past to direct yourself to a better future.
149. Never let the Adversary make you doubt God's forgiveness. When you have this temptation, remember these things:
    - "He has not dealt with us according to our sins, nor punished us

according to our iniquities" (Psalm 103:10).
- What the Father did with the prodigal son (Luke 15).

150. Never provide a service or advice unless:
- You are asked.
- You ask if they need your help.
- The Lord Jesus always asks, "Do you want to be healed?" Though He can heal all, He asks first.

151. Never speak in a weak way.
- Because God is your source of power.
- The pity of anyone will not make you strong.

152. Never forget a decision that you made during your hardship.
- This forgetting may drive you to another hardship.

153. Never open a needle-sized hole to the Adversary in your life.
- Today it is the size of a needle; you can close it, but you do not want to.
- Tomorrow, it will be a big gate that you want to close but cannot.
- The needle-sized hole is like one cigarette or one beer; the big gate is like addiction and alcoholism.

154. Never smoke.
- It is unwise behavior that you know can harm you, but you do it anyway.

- Never be deceived by the ad that says, "Great savings—buy two packs and get one free."
- The true great saving is saving your life and your money.

155. Never boast about your deeds.
    - Do not open the eyes of the Adversary to tempt your success.
    - Remember: "Happy is he who does not condemn himself in what he approves" (Roman 14:22).

156. Never give more information than what you are asked.

157. Never admit a bad thought.
    - Instead, hope for a better one.
    - Acknowledging bad thoughts magnifies them.

158. Never be trapped in what people say about you.
    - The best you can do will not please people.
    - The least you can do will please God.
    - It is your choice which one you want to please.

159. Never complain to your family or a friend about your spouse.
    - Their advice will favor you, and not your spouse.
    - This will worsen the situation.

160. Never take "no" as an answer from one you know is capable of saying "yes."

- Some people do not want to work or do not know how to answer, and they use "no" as a standard response that excuses them from doing anything.
- Make a reasonable effort to get a real answer from the person—or at least some direction from them about where you can find the answer to your question.

161. Never waste your time in anger and anxiety.
- Life is too short.
- Flip the coin; instead of a destructive emotion, choose a constructive one.

162. Never let a bad professor makes you hate a class or the material.
- If you know he is bad, why let him affect your life?

163. Never correct a man who has the wrong standards.
- No matter what you say, it will not fit into his idea of what is right.
- If you have to do so, just say, "Is it right to do this?" or "Is it acceptable by God to do this?" and then leave him with his conscience.

164. Never exercise on Sunday morning.
- You have all week to go to the gym.
- This is the time you need to exercise your spirit in church.

165. Never follow popular preference simply because it's popular.

- It is not always right.
166. Never drive close behind a big truck.
     - You will not see the traffic light.
     - If it is yellow and you cannot see
       it because you are too close to the
       truck and the truck blocks out the
       traffic light, by the time you realize
       it, you have just gone through a red
       light.
167. Never say to your son, "You did better than I
     expected."
     - You don't want him to feel that you
       expect him not to do well.
168. Never discipline your son in front of
     people.
169. Never say it is a bad day to do something.
     - Instead, say it's not the right day to
       do this.
170. Never say, "I fear."
     - Instead, "God willing everything will
       be fine."
171. Never say, "I do not care."
     - It is better to say, "It is not my
       concern at this point."
     - You care because you are a sincere
       person, but there are priorities.
172. Never say, "To be honest."
     - You should be honest all the time,
       not just now with the person you are
       talking to.
173. Never say, "I do not trust anyone."

- Instead, "I trust everyone, but I do not trust the Adversary who pushes people to do bad things."

174. Never say, "It is not my job."
    - Instead, "Let me see who can help you better than I can."

175. Never forget your wife's birthday, and never remember her age.

176. Never think having this or that will make you happy.
    - If you are not happy now, the way you are, nothing will make you happy.

177. Never forget to smile before you walk into work.

178. Never turn on your sprinkler when rain is in the forecast.

179. Never wonder about those who are sick and challenged in life.
    - Help them; pray for them.
    - But remember God has His own business with His creation.

180. Never bend at the waist to lift a heavy object; bend your knees instead and keep your back totally straight.
    - You want to keep a healthy back.
    - Find an assistance tool in these situations.

181. Never hire cheap movers.
    - These extra few hundred dollars may save your valuable furniture.

182. Never think of just yourself after you marry.

- Think of two; when your wife is pregnant, then think of three.

183. Never open your garage door when you're still far away from it.
     - Wait until you get closer, so that the vibration of the car will make lizards and other unwelcome visitors run away instead of running into the garage.

184. Never buy a new house as soon as you get a promotion.
     - First pay off your debts before you increase them.

185. Never start a relationship or friendship when you are stressed or have disturbed emotions.

186. Never be stingy with your money if you are blessed with it.
     - Help others, and that will help you in eternity.
     - You cannot take your money with you to heaven; it is invalid currency.
     - However, good deeds are valid currency in heaven.

187. Never depend on your supervisor's verbal instructions to know your job description.
     - You must read your job description.

188. Never expect that your parenting responsibilities will ever end.
     - This job is a forever position with no retirement plan and no promotion,

but if you do it right, you will be very successful.
- Its magnificent rewards are seeing your children happy and having a good life.

189. Never calm your crying son in the back seat when you are driving.
- Your safety and his are important.
- The best you can do is to sing his favorite song until he calms down.

190. Never waste time and energy in a relationship whose conclusion is uncertain.

191. Never forget your hat and your sunglasses when you go to the beach.

192. Never sign the back of your credit card.
- Always write "see ID."
- If you lose your card, you lose it with your signature as well.

193. Never get frustrated when you drive behind a senior citizen who is driving slowly.
- One day you will reach this age, and you would not want anyone to rush you.

194. Never think that God loves your neighbor or your co-worker more than you because they have a bigger house or a nicer car.
- God's love is not shown in material things alone.
- God gives many blessings that are not seen.

195. Never buy anything online from an unknown company without first checking

the Better Business Bureau website and customer reports for the product.

196. Never forget to confirm that the two rooms are next to each other when you reserve a vacation with your family.

197. Never say that all inventions are already made.
    - You may invent something new.

198. Never think of work outside of work.
    - Especially when you are on vacation.

199. Never agree to extract a tooth unless at least two dentists have told you that's the only option.

200. Never replenish the calories that you burn in exercise, but always replenish the water that you lost.

201. Never let your teenager stay outside the house after curfew.
    - This will keep him safe until he has wisdom.
    - Then when he has wisdom, he will know to be at the right place at the right time.

202. Never leave your convertible open in the parking lot.
    - You never know when it is going to rain.

203. Never get offended with how people treat you; they may not even know how to treat themselves.

204. Never get upset on your day off.

- It is your day to relax.

205. Never say to anyone, "You should not do this."
     - Not all people accept advice.
     - You can say, "It may be a good idea to do this."

206. Never say, "I have many things to do," especially in the morning.
     - Saying this at the beginning of your day will make the Adversary push against you in accomplishing what you want.
     - If you want to accomplish things, move silently.

207. Never get hurt by words.

208. Never worry about who is Mr. or Ms. Right.
     - Ask the Big Matchmaker, God.

209. Never take your work stress home with you.

210. Never get married before at least six months of engagement.
     - Your work required three letters of recommendation to hire you.
     - You need three documents to secure this marriage:
       ☐ Background report.
       ☐ Lab work.
       ☐ Church membership.
     - Before all of these, you need God's approval.

211. Never underestimate your two-year-old and let him/her play with nail polish or lipstick.

- It is likely to end up on your walls and floors.
- However, if it happens, smile about it because it is their way of expressing their creativity.

212. Never let the Adversary push you to do something that you do not have peace about.
     - If you have peace, be sure that it is the divine peace.

213. Never let your mind be disturbed by someone who hurt you.
     - Just remember this: "Forgive us our trespasses as we forgive those who trespass against us."

214. Never repay evil with evil.
     - Those who do evil are deceived by the Adversary to hurt another human.

215. Never try something that another man has tried and told you is bad.
     - Drugs and alcohol are examples.

216. Never ignore the advice of your parents and grandparents.
     - They love you and do not want to see you get hurt.
     - It is true that we have more technology in our day than they did, but the principles of life are the same.

217. Never forget to put the gift receipt with the gift.

      - The recipient may want to exchange it for something else.

218. Never believe the Adversary, who lies to you and tells you that if you go to God with your sins, He will not accept you. Remember these two things:

      - "The one who comes to Me I will by no means cast out" (John 6:37).

      - "Who desires all men to be saved and to come to the knowledge of the truth" (1 Timothy 2:4).

219. Never complain about your job. The Adversary will know about it and make you hate it more.

      - To cool yourself down, consider what you would do if you did not have a job.

220. Never call without leaving a message.

      - How many relationships would have been resolved if a message had been left?

      - When leaving your phone number on someone's voicemail, make sure to include your area code and repeat it twice (a little slower the second time).

221. Never think that your needs are beyond God's ability.

      - Remember: "Who is able to do exceedingly abundantly above all that we ask or think, according to the power that works in us" (Ephesians 3:20).

222. Never refer success to yourself. Remember this:
   - "God who works in you both to will and to do for His good pleasure" (Philippians 2:13).
   - "He who gives you power to get wealth, that He may establish His covenant which He swore to your fathers" (Deuteronomy 8:18).

223. Never use ketchup without shaking the bottle first.

224. Never assume the water faucets in public restrooms will behave the same way they do in your house.
   - Sometimes the water pressure is so high that, if you're not careful, you will get splashed with water when you turn the water on.

225. Never forget to adjust the mirrors when you're driving someone else's car.

226. Never grill with nice clothes on.

227. Never forget proof of your child's age when traveling with a "lap infant."
   - Make sure to have your child's birth certificate or his or her passport.
   - Doing this will allow you to avoid two issues:
     - ☐ Uncooperative travel agents who want you buy a ticket for your infant.

☐ Stubborn security officers who want you to prove the child's identity.

228. Never forget your neck pillow on a long trip.
229. Never enter a conversation between a man and his wife even if you are the best friend.
230. Never give up on your family.
    - Forgive your family members for their mistakes and do not focus on errors they may have made in the past.
    - Letting them know you forgive them can change their lives and yours.
231. Never accept information without analyzing it.
    - This will make you focus on what is important; figure out what is wrong.
    - Make sure your information is coming from a reputable source.
232. Never forget to teach your wife how to change a tire.
    - It will be handy when you are out of town or unable to help her.
233. Never over-do baby-proofing.
    - God keeps children safe and protected.
    - Our grandparents survived without recent technologies.
234. Never believe all TV commercials.
    - Ask a friend who has tried it before you dare to buy it.
235. Never forget to laugh at a joke that you've heard many times.

- Laughter will lift your mood.
- Appreciate the person who tried to make you laugh.

236. Never stay in bed once you are awake.
- Staying in bed with no sleep makes negative thoughts creep into your brain.

237. Never let your teenager travel internationally with another teenager or by himself.

238. Never leave anything that you can do today for tomorrow.
- Tomorrow has its own things.

239. Never let your big bank account inflate your ego.
- Remember we came naked to this world, and we leave it naked as well.
- Remember it is God who gave you that big bank account and He can take it away.

240. Never think that God hates you when you are facing a serious health condition.
- It is just a turning point in your life.
- All things happen for a reason; even something that seems bad at the time.

241. Never say, "I am alone."
- Remember He said, "I am with you always" (Matthew 28:20).

242. Never let the Adversary mess with your mind.
- Your pitfalls start there.

243. Never play lotto.

- The love of money is the root of all evil.
- Fast money makes the mind lose its balance.

244. Never fall into the habit of eating in front of TV.
    - It is the beginning of being obese.
    - You need to enjoy your food.

245. Never expose a disagreement between you and your spouse in front of your children.
    - This has a negative and deep effect on their subconscious.

246. Never allow any of your family to speak a negative word about your spouse.

247. Never hurt your wife's feelings.
    - God gave her to you as a gift.
    - Hurting her feelings means that you have no gratefulness for God's gift.

248. Never allow your expenses to be greater than 80% of your income.
    - Remember: 10% tithe and 10% savings.

249. Never study with a slacker who refuses your encouragement.

250. Never correct nor criticize your spouse's family except through your spouse.
    - They can bear their son/daughter's words.
    - Keep your relationship with them pure.
    - Make sure that your spouse does this in a positive way.

Conclusion

I hope you will add to these suggestions on the pages that follow and then give this book to the next generation so that they may have wisdom to succeed and proceed in life.

Never forget that with every "always" and "never" there are some exceptions. It is God's wisdom that enables us to discern when to say "always" and when to say "never."

I hope that this book finds its way to your heart and adds something positive to your life. May God bless you always.

About the Author

Malak Morgan was trained in Egypt as a medical doctor and practiced medicine there for three years. He immigrated to the United States in March 1999. After recovering from a challenging heart condition, through strong faith in the Lord Jesus Christ, he continued his education. He received his Doctorate of Pharmacy from the University of Florida College of Pharmacy.

Malak is thrilled to combine clinical knowledge, spiritual principles, and everyday guidelines into a simple message that can inspire everyone. His passion is to search into the human soul and divine wisdom. His message is how to overcome life's challenges and overcome the traps of the Adversary through the divine power of God.

Always & Never is his first published work. He has copyrighted a few literary works and there will be more to come in the future. He is optimistic that he can make a difference in the lives of his readers and improve their quality of life. His favorite moments are watching the purity of a child's smile and blessing his Creator, God. He is a deacon in the Coptic Orthodox Christian Church. He has been married to Monica since 2006 and has two sons, Joseph and Jacob.

Always

Always

_____

_____

_____

_____

_____

_____

_____

_____

_____

_____

_____

_____

_____

_____

_____

_____

_____

_____

_____

_____

_____

_____

_____

Always

Always

Never

_____

_____

_____

_____

_____

_____

_____

_____

_____

_____

_____

_____

_____

_____

_____

_____

_____

_____

_____

_____

_____

_____

_____

Never

_____

_____

_____

_____

_____

_____

_____

_____

_____

_____

_____

_____

_____

_____

_____

_____

_____

_____

_____

_____

_____

Never

Never

_____
_____
_____
_____
_____
_____
_____
_____
_____
_____
_____
_____
_____
_____
_____
_____
_____
_____
_____
_____
_____
_____
_____
_____
_____